Living Land Publishing
www.livingland.wales
Pembrokeshire, Wales UK

Printed by Cleddau Press Ltd. Haverfordwest,
Pembrokeshire, SA61 2JE

Cover image www.pixabay.com
Photo P77 Peter Knight
Photo P24 www.pixabay.com
All other photos Julie and Tim Kirby

To Sara & Jonathan

Living
Crumbs

Poems and prayers

Much love

Julie xx

Julie Kirby

Dedicated to Tim,
With all my love and gratitude.

Contents

Prayers

Introduction

One of my early memories is sitting in my grandmother's house, by the fire on a wet school holiday, writing some long -winded story about a girl travelling through Europe. At the time I wrote a lot of little tales and even simple poems. It was something that was so frequent for me as to go unnoticed and unremarked upon; little poems or stories and then later in adulthood I'd write blogs. But mostly they were private musings or just something simple – it never occurred that I should share them wider, or even keep them for any length of time. I don't know what happened to that first story.

It was only in training to be an Interfaith Minister, a process embarked upon in 2017, that my true voice

appeared. I had ceremonies, prayers and other assignments to write. Sometimes I'd sit in quiet, seemingly in communion with a blank page or a windy hilltop and words and phrases would form.
This is how the poems began...

Even now, I can't say where the ideas come from, whether they are me or something beyond me.
I don't think it matters.
But, I am infused with gratitude that somehow I've been gifted ideas that I then put into some sort of order.

I then learned to give the words to others, firstly within the loving embrace of my fellow students and tutors during the course and then on to Facebook in live readings. Very gently, I started opening myself out to the sharing of these words. I needed much gentle encouragement to share what was so tender and often quite personal.

Eventually the idea of putting my poems together in to a book seemed like a good idea, but I remember feeling extremely daunted. There was so much to think of in terms of how I envisioned the project. Not just the obvious; what to put in and what to leave out. But also how I should order the work, how I wanted the pages to look, the photos, the font, the styling.
And yet throughout this process the most important consideration was how I wanted you to feel into the essence of these words – what was I trying to convey in these pages. How could I take you on a journey that lifted you in to the vision I could see.
Writing poems seemed the easy bit somehow.

But I've always believed that our greatest learning is just outside the comfort zone. So I've leaned into that difficulty, and gently, but with powerful faith slowly forged ahead. So with much

encouragement from Tim and much
coffee, it is done.
A physical book!
Imagine that...
And now you, Dear Reader sit with this
book in your hands.
It is done!
And, as I sit at my desk writing this
introduction, looking out on the sea
and mountains of West Wales; with the
rain falling softly down the window I am
thinking of you.
Know that in this moment we are
united through the type and the paper.
How wonderful!
I wish you many blessings as you turn
the pages.

Reverend Julie
September 2020
julie@livingland.wales

Poems

The Calling

Into the landscape we are led
Feeling heart strong and opening.
It senses our boots, our scent.
We feel into the rocks and mountains,
Called by the sea song hush of the
coast.

Come.
     Come.

Fly with your possessions few and land
on these shores.
Track to house where you will reside.

Come.
     Come.

Be beyond human rules and laws
To blend into the grass and gorse.
Soar as you are meant to with wings of
ravens

Speak for the ancient ones on whose
bones you tread.
Live as one with the elements and
dragons.

Come.
     Come.

N^{ow}

Rush
Fast
Go
Forward
One-way
Speed
Gallop
Heart-rate
Panic!

Breath...
Slow
Stop
Stand-still
Circle
Pause
Walk
Birdsong
Live...

Ripples

A stone's throw away
Interconnected action.
Growing effect from one little splash
Circles overlapping.
Can one small stone do all that?
Is that my effect?
Will one toe in the water cause that
connection?
Fleeting patterns
Growing out yet fading.
All returns to calm
With me still there
And the water is cooling and refreshing.

Drought

Parched earth
Cracks appear
Gaping mouths
Chapped for want of liquid.

At last the rain comes.
Gushing
Flooding
Greening
Refreshed closed tongues.

Fluffed soil
Spattered paths
Drenched earth.

Inspire

Dark living earth grounds and anchors
the bare feet that tread the path.
Deeply living crumbs.

Water connects all to sea and blood,
drenching through a purity to be
absorbed.

Air ruffles feathers and fur and hair.
Breathing the one oxygen that all
connects.

The shimmer of fire flames, fans the
energy within.
We thirstily drink of its power.

Dappled sparkles of light from sun and
self,
Warms the bones and inner spirals.
Coursing love through cells,
Soaking all with grace.

Mindspace

Racing down corridors, looking in
doors.
Babble of people in the endless noise.
Hurtling through the labyrinth
Searching for peace.
Cluttered storage in corners –
everywhere.

At last, at the end
A creaky door opens.
Spirit soars
Sky for ceiling
Grounding earth for floor
No walls.
Fresh breeze
To breathe
Think
Be.

March

Sparklingly bright today
Birds singing, in on the scam.
For the sun is in league with the icy
wind.
Step out ungloved and it'll whip fingers
crackingly sore.

A cruel trick, a promise of warmth
beckons you through double glazed
windows.
We are so isolated from the elements
hermetically sealed like an out of date
pasty.

Smells of spring today.
A fresh laundered feeling
Tinglingly sharp in the nose.
Not the artificial washo/spray scent,
But of nature new and unwrapped.
To mask this is to lose yet another
connection with all around us.

Another lost sense.
But how many people can still breathe
it?

Soft green of new growth today.
Unfurling buds on rain blackened tree
twigs.
Show promise and faith in the summer
to come.

For now the hats are pulled down low
and the trudge is a quick one.
Who has noticed these tiny unfurlings?
Who has stroked the soft down of the
bud covers?
Do you even allow a moment from your
phone to look?

The artificial seems brighter than all
around us.
We have lost the subtlety, the softness,
the senses.
The wonder.
We are wholly lost.
We must return.....

Home blessing

The depth of stones holds the space of
home.
Let the songs of life dress the walls.

The strength of beams brace the storms
that rain.
Let the cries of all bead the ceiling.

The earthen ground holds tales of
ancestors.
Let the steadfastness of the sweeping
one draw paths through the floor.

The abundance of garden rooted and
leafed within.
Let the well of water broth give life to all
creatures.

The fire hearthed yet wildly dancing;
tamed for the now.
Let love spark glow through all
elements, gods and mortals.

Serenity

Serenity is a Sunday afternoon
Warm and snoozy after lunch.

Serenity is gazing long into the garden pond
And watching frenzied tadpoles dart.

Serenity is a country house, centuries old
And weathered with love.

Serenity is understanding the age you are
And neither trying to capture your youth or wanting to..

The Windowsill

I have a thinking spot in my house.
A place of contemplation and reflection.
A lovely view across the gardens.
Nothing to distract me,
No rush of traffic.
Just a few pigeons in the trees
and the cats stalking below.

I can stare from this window for ages,
Lost in my thoughts.
Solving my problems.
Watching nothing happening.
No sound through the window.
Just the creak and hum of an old house
behind me.

Washing Line

There is a deep honesty in a full
washing line.
Our linen, jeans and socks airing in the
breeze.
Or hanging limply in the drizzle that
was supposed to be merely a passing
shower.
Instead its stuck around to give an
extra penitent rinse.

Washing on the line is timeless.
It speaks of sleeves rolled up,
Of labour and muscles stretching back
into the arms of our grandmothers and
beyond.
As long as we've dressed we've washed
our clothes.

It hints at starting again.
Of sweat and stains absolved in the
communion of water and soap.

Renewal in a clean shirt.
Revival of a use-softened bib.
Resurrection of a t-shirt.

There will be the promise of sun
scented towels for all and crisp bed
sheets tonight.
Folded abundance in wardrobes and
drawers
Of nature captured in warp and weft
Stitch and loop
That unique scent of light and air that
wraps our bodies with timeless honesty.

Fireside

Guardian flames crackle and spit
Dancing heat
Orange
Crimson
Sentinel.

Rain rages outside
Demanding to be let in
To wetten and darken the walls.
Ashen
Haggardly
Primal.

We sit
You and I
In that flickering cave warmth
Of sofas and books and tea
Cocooned quietly amongst ourselves
Sinking deep into to the cushions
And our love.

Microcosm

Single storey mosses meander
through sky scraping blades of straight
green grass.

Daisy domes offer shelter from raindrop
globes.
Some insects will only know a daisy
from the green cupped white underside.
They may never have experienced the
yellow medal above.

Industrious ants commute hurriedly
Whilst great armoured beetles trundle
across uneven earth pavements.
They never trip and they never sue.

Striped yarn balls of bees land on the
shards of dandelion platters
The yellows almost matching.
Other flying things land near vertically
with a skill we've barely mastered.

And beneath all, the worms trail
mystical blind wisdom
Silent creators of nourishment for the
chain of life.

A whole society in microcosm
with life and death
Abundance and disaster
Within a square foot of what we
humans call a lawn
And they sense as home.

L ament of a Field Mouse

Fear my blood cells
Speed my muscles
Rustle in the grass?
Wasn't me.
I was elsewhere.
Buzzard wing shadow
I hide still..
Nowhere is safe
I trust no being
Not even the seed eating
All fickle
Danger of teethed snout that probes my
night
Terror!
Quick resolve.
But my small existence
invalid suddenly.

Song of a Bird Soul

Drifting
    Soaring
        Banking
Wings outstretched.
Drifting
    Soaring
Beak wide.
Calling praise
    Calling anguish on flight.
Plummeting
Earth rising to sky
Peak stone brushing.
Calling still
Lifting
    Twirling
        Spinning
Wings outstretched.
    Plaintive
        Ruffled freedom.
Soaring
Playing on thermals

Spirals and circles
Plummet again
Cries!
        Too fast
Fading of light
Shadows lengthening

Nothing remains but an earthly pile of
feathers dispersing with the breeze...

Soaking up the Skylarks' song

My shoes don't match the horse's prints
They smile their horseshoe curve in the
mud.

Insects beg pardon as they crash into
me,
bouncing onwards jauntily,
weaving across the vast plain of the
track
Travelling into the microcosm of the
hedgerow.

I plod on, legs automatic
I forget I'm walking,
seemingly propelled forward.
Distance being travelled
Hedgerow evolving.

Soaking up the skylarks' song
Crescendo-ing around the fields
The birds not visible.

Risen song streaming back to the earth
of striped crops
Greening of land in uniform rows
Swords of infant wheat raised to meet
the notes.

The blinding yellow of oil seed rape
dazzling the slopes of the distance.
We seem to have accepted the
interloper.
It bridges the gold gap between daffodils
and dandelions.
Charging the sunlight.

And still the skylarks infuse the air
Volume tuned to combine with bass of
lamb and ewe in the daisy flecked next
field.
A buzzard mews on a thermal.

It is all above me and surrounding me
Sound and song, sight and colour.
I could be in any year and any century.
I am a lone human in a spring sprung,
joyously sunshine drunk world.
I soak up the skylarks a little more.

Three Poems for the Covid-19 Pandemic of 2020

Distance

Shoreside the air is still sweet with
salty blessings.
Beach stretching sideways.
Dune crescent mirroring Luna pull of
tide.

I am a singular black long dot as I walk
in the distance.
Tangly coarse grasses in their
minimalist way tie the great sand bank
to rock,
Weaving jewels of sea thrift as they go.
Prayer hands folds of giant alien slate
slabs
Stretching bonily with limpet gnarls
pleading supplications to the seagulls
who cry sermons overhead.

There is a fearful distance in our
stance, but not in our polite shouts to
each other above the crashing waves.

Aloneness – what the sea does best.
Its moodiness means it is not always
good or safe company.
It is our wildest neighbour.
Within the new rules we crave its
anarchy and tumbling abandon.
Marine drops of life surge together to
blanket the pebbles.
No distancing of water here.

Back home and lock the door
The tide turns without us to witness it.
As it always has.
The world spins
As it always has.
As if nothing has happened.

Timeless

And to the stones we shall return.
When it is permitted.
And time means nothing to the
landscape.

Crags look out through
Sunsets and dawns,
Solstices and darkness,
Cycles and spirals.

Nothing really changing.
All seen.
All understood.
In a depth that forges a bond
Between bluestone and bedrock,
Rain and tides,
Peaks and stars.

Clouds painting shapes across fields
As they have always amused
themselves.

Sand grains slipping silkily over dune
fingers
As they have always loved.
Chattering grasses selling secrets
across the heathland
As they have always said.

Nothing really changing.
All seen.
All understood.
In a depth that forges a bond

All without human softness and
fragility.
We forget our place.
We are not timeless and that tragedy is
unnoticed.

Go within

Leave the supermarket crush and the
warnings on the news.
Go within.

At your home open the door and the
cupboards and see all that you have.
The abundance of warmth and
provisions
But do not tarry here
Go within.
Take off your boots and fill your water
glass
Hurry to your room and shut the door.
Go within.

Sit in your best chair, lean back into its
supporting role.
Your feet are grounded on wood or
carpet, but beneath the manmade the
earth is still there anchoring you.

Gaze softly at the way the window
frames the garden
But do not tarry here.
Go within.
Breathe
Just breathe
So that that and the ticking clock are
the only sounds.
Go within.

Drop down from your head of worries
and headlines
Ssh them as you would a child to sleep.
Go within.
Land softly down in the dark womb of
your heart
Settle there.
Breathe
You are so safe
You are so at peace
You are home
You are within.

Feel the tiny flutter of Hope
Never crush its beautiful wings

Be held safely by Compassion
Like the tenderest of maternal hugs.
Breathe
Be soothed
You are within.

The essence of you is the light you can
see.
It never flickers or dims.
It is not a lonely light.
You are connected to All that is Hope
All that is Compassion
And All that is Love.
Breathe.
You are home
You are within.

The light is Love.
It is You!
It is Divine.
You are all these things
Hope, Compassion and Love.
But then your head knew this
Your heart knew this
Outside made you forget.
You are safe.

You are at peace
You are home
You are within.

Stay.
Breathe.
Feel love
Feel all these wonderful things
Feed that light of Love.
Stretch out your arms to send
Compassion to your poor human self
and all others huddled in fear.
Infuse all with love.
Gently give Hope space to fly
Go Within.

Let the joy rise in you

Whatever pushed you to your knees in
the mud has now passed.
You have been dragged through the
blood and piss
And been washed so thoroughly as to
not recognise yourself.
But it is leaving you.
Changed.

Staggering to your knees after the
tsunami of grief and pain
Look – you've travelled that far!
Changed.

Look how life has pushed you
Wipe your mouth dry of screams.
Your hands are still attached!
Still strongly gripped on to life and
living.

Stand now.
Your feet are still anchored to Earth
You've not been thrown off.
Let the breeze softly rock you.

There is a tingle – quiet at first.
Can you sense it?
It fizzes and sparkles almost
imperceptibly, through the muscles of
your legs and upwards.
Gathering as it goes.

Your strength is returning.
And how strong you are!
Open your arms wide to that strength.
Feel the power move through all your
being.
Fuel of love.

Let the joy rise in you!
And out through your smile
And in the glitter of your eyes.
Birds' wingbeat applauds from above.
Smile at the blueness of flowers
Wink at trees' leaf bound praise.
Strong joyful sap in your bones.

But there are now budding wings on
your back.
New and freshly unsheathed.
Gently flutter them open
Let them dry in the warm sun.

Wild Peace

Wild peace of the waves rolling and
chorusing foam on the sands.

Pebbles shuffled and falling gripped by
water that drags them to reshaping.

Gales sing the song of ancestors
through the cracks in the windows
Chasing deep notes down organ pipe
chimneys.

Birds wheel and dance around their
castle crag hill tops
Holding the fort of forever and back.

This is the elemental peace of always
Unchanged by internet or bright
sodium lights.

This speaks to the wild peace of
belonging.

To earth and sky
Gorse and wren
Stone and stream.

To the unchanging loving darkness of
the heart
Soul of wild peace.

Raven Black

Raven black.
Wings buzzard soaring on thermals
playing
Calling your wisdom from the weight of
twigs.

Raven black
Wholeness sharp brain of mystery and
knowing
Loyal to mate and fort of craggy heights.

Raven black
Speak the moon and sun two worlds
woven
See all with guard beak of gratitude
unspoken.

Raven black
Glisten of jet eye whilst rooks still
gossip

Shimmer of feather cloak covers sky in passing.
Seer, seeker, priest and Merlin.

Raven black.

Journey

Pause between worlds where the sky is
down and the earth cries tears of
belonging.

Climb the life tree and bark step pull to
the mist.
Leaf green brightness with lichen
fingers grasp.
Guides see you and beckon.

Climb the life tree and branch where
the wind calls.
Cleave the heart open that love may
hear your soul wrenched to be rejoined.

Soar the life tree and lift beyond body
enchantment.
Drift between worlds where the journey
speaks and gratitude kisses feather
down rest

Descend the life tree and feet retrace
nest hollows.

Thank the drum and the heartbeat
Follow the path home.

Stormus

The gale disturbs the smooth cloak of
the blackbird.
Suddenly it's tattered and ragged.
Sea snarling in the harbour
Caged against the high walls.
It calls for freedom and wild abandon
from order of brick and rope.

I feel the power of the elements
Dark clouds holding back the rumble of
thunder.
Pent up
Rain imprisoned momentarily.
Electricity in my cells matching the
cells of the lightening.

To be outside is to feel raw passions of
wind fingers grasping my hair.
Pulling
Tugging
Lusting to take me with it.

Tasting sea salt kisses
Uprooting me from soggy ground.

Where to – my beloved?
Where shall we go?

To the hill tops where ravens dwell
Calling for the lost ones at sea.
To the water where I'd be dragged to the
depths.
Never to kiss again.
To the sky to feel my smooth cloak
tattered and ragged.
To dwell in the heart of clouds that is
nowhere.

Where to-my beloved?
Where shall we go?

To the storm of lifeforce
From fingers whipped of fire.
To the thunder of tears
To the lightening spark of life.

I do not shelter from the storm
In the plastic box of forgetting.

But stand in my glory
As one with my ancestors' reality.
Drenched
Tugged
Dishevelled
Spent
Held by wind's wild passions
To rest on the earth again.

Seasons

Autumn
Undoing summer
Trees ablaze
Undercover toadstools
Mists and woody scents
Numbing nature death.

Winter
Icy Blasts
Never ending rain
Tinsel frosts
Empty earth
Real fire warmth.

Spring
Precious new growth
Reborn life
In uplifting praise
Nodding daffodils
Gleaming clean light.

Summer
Utterly balmy warmth
More ice-cream please
Marigold yellow
Endless evening
Relaxing sun.

Only when

Only when you are still enough will you
sense the earth's heartbeat.
Be still.

Only when you are un-encumbered will
the wind's breath match yours
And mine.
Be free.

Only when you hear the song of the
stones will your heart soar in connected
longing.
Be listening.

Only when you run your fingers
through the grass stalks will you feel
life caress you in return.
Be loving.

Only when you taste the rain in the air
will you be washed of troubles.
Be open.

Only when you allow the sun to kiss
your head top will it all make sense.
Be kissed.

Only..
Be

Only when..
Be

Only then..
Be

40

She reached the next pinnacle and
stopped to admire the view.
The last climb had been easy, full of fun
and laughter.
In the far distance she could see the
peaks of childhood and teenage and the
varied terrain between.
The crevasse of broken hearts and
sorrow, the rolling warm plains of joy.

Scattered along her path were a few
graves of emotions she'd left.
Shyness was buried by a blooming
flower of confidence.
Naivety also a grey slab.
The wisdom flower she carried like a
staff, ever-growing as her guide.
Herself too had blossomed from gawky
slim twigs into rounded branches
etched with living.

By her side ran the path of her beloved.
So nice to have company now.
Although being older, she was ahead of
him in conquest, their paths were
intertwined with happiness and love.
She turned in the warm of contentment
and looked to the future.
Unmapped and unknown trails lay
ahead, vague distant peaks just visible;
Intangible and unetched.
All cloaked in the heady clouds of
destiny.

Breath of a Dragon

From before written time there are tales
of dragons.
Creatures of wind and fire and water.
For they are as the elements and as real
as the sky and the stars.

They have flown as heroes and villains,
adversaries and guides.
They are without past folk century and
without future invention.

But now deep, deep within the earth
and rocks of the Welsh mountains it is
said that the dragons are sleeping.

Sometimes when you can see a little
cloud sat just on the craggy highest
peak – then know that is whisper of a
dragon's breath.
They are silent beneath the ancient
peaks.

They are cooled within the springs of
the mountains.
They are hibernating and are still as the
rocks that surround them.

Dragons sleep until they know there is
a need for their wisdom and their
power.
Dragons dream until they know there is
a need for their fire and air.

Dragons wait..
Dragons hold...
Dragons are still...

But sometimes the world turns, and
they stretch a wing.
The earth rumbles and they open one
great eye.
A whisper reaches them, and a claw is
extended.
Rain beats ahead and they know the
time is approaching.
They unfurl, unfold, uncoil and
unwrap.

Shaking great heads at the folly around
them.
Dragon tears fall fizzing on the stones of
their bed.
Vast wings spreading up through crags
and gullies.
Great ribs open to intake of dragon
breath from sky to heart hearth
outbreath of fire.
They reach upwards through the
depths of their earth beds.

Wisdom of another age is needed now.
Will you call them?

Wisdom of the warrior.
Will you stand alongside?

Wisdom of the dragon.
Will you fly with them?

Taking up your own wings and soaring
on the winds of the stars.
Swooping down amongst the greatest
seas.

Banking through ancient forests and
deserts.
Swirling and twirling.
Great flapping of scales and
membranes powering you globe-wards
and on.

Will you fly with a dragon?
Drawing fiery energy from your own
heart to power you.
Radiating beyond your physical form.

To a dragon, your body is nothing.
To a dragon, you are beyond your
human self.
To a dragon, you are Divine
Feel dragon pull you upwards to the
deep strength of your own being.
your root to earth, your thread to stars.
Your heart to blinding bright love.
Your full powerful truth.

You are your own dragon –
Face your reflection in rain's pools.
See your vast and powerful wings.

See your great tail ready to sweep all behind you.
See your fiery breath speak your truth.
Draw yourself to your great height.
Unfurl your wings to their full majesty and glory.
And fly.

But until the dragons are needed, deep, deep within the earth and rocks of the Welsh mountains it is said that the dragons are sleeping.

Trilogy of One

Be in the silence and listen.
Close our eyes and see.
Touch the centre of our being
Leaving no fingerprints.
Taste the truth of who we are.
Balance our thoughts with stardust,
Calm our muscles with rain.
Let the fire of the sunset draw us
upwards
To flow to the sea again.
We do not need our earthly senses to
meet the truth of ourselves.
We are as real as granite
As soft as a petal
As strong as a storm.
We are as humble as the greatest oak
And as wise as the bees.
We Are One.

Be in the silence and listen.
Close your eyes and see.
Touch the centre of your being
Leaving no fingerprints.
Taste the truth of who you are.
Balance your thoughts with stardust
Calm your muscles with rain.
Let the fire of the sunset draw you
upwards
To flow to the sea again.
You do not need your earthly senses to
meet the truth of yourself.
You are as real as granite
As soft as a petal
As strong as a storm.
You are as humble as the greatest oak
And as wise as the bees.
You Are One.

Be in the silence and listen.
Close my eyes and see.
Touch the centre of my being
Leaving no fingerprints.
Taste the truth of who I am.
Balance my thoughts with stardust,
Calm my muscles with rain.
Let the fire of the sunset draw me
upwards
To flow to the sea again.
I do not need my earthly senses to meet
the truth of myself.
I am as real as granite
As soft as a petal
As strong as a storm.
I am as humble as the greatest oak
And as wise as the bees.
I Am One.

Inner Me

Catch my energy
Chase my spirit
Let me dance.
Don't make me sit down not even for a
minute.

See the light that sparkles from within
How could you want to snuff it?
Or fade it to dim?

I laugh
I run
I bounce and play

This is ME
Let me inspire
Don't push it away.

Love Is

Love is not...

Possession
Anger
Power
Hurt
Pain
Lies
Blind.

Love is...

Touching
Gentle
Talking
Free
Tender
Sharing
Whole.

You Are Loved

You are loved.
No matter the label you apply to
yourself,
Or others apply to you.

You are loved.
Seen.
As you are
All of You.

No need to close the petals of your
shadows.
I see them.
And love you still.

When you are anguished and cry
prayers in the infinity of the darkness
I hear them.
And love you still.

You are loved.
No matter the trouble you apply to
yourself,
Or others apply to you.

You are loved.
Seen.
As you are
All of You.

When small triumphs of thinking or
doing go unnoticed around you
I hear them.
And love you still.

You are loved
For I am You.

Beyond Words

Beyond words is another world
Illegible
Experiential.
Uncatchable in mere arrangement of
squiggles called letters.

See it
Not with my eyes
But with my heart.

Hear it
Not with my ears
But with the depth of my being.

It calls
Beyond words.

Step but not with feet
Choose but not with logic
Open my senses beyond the pen and
paper.

80

Beyond flesh
Beyond bone
Beyond words.

I cannot recall that which is not
governed by time.
I cannot process that which is not of
order.

In that boundless darkness I exist
towards the brightest of lights.
In that world I sense the
fathomlessness of love.

Beyond words
I cannot bring it back through the
portal of paper.
I cannot draw it with flowery
descriptions and clever rhymes.

Yet it calls
And I am drawn
Beyond words.

Prayers

Prayers Introduction

As a foreword to this section of the book on prayers and before we delve into what prayer may be, it's really important that I clarify my position on the nature of the Divine.

I am an Interfaith Minister and as such it is not for me to convince you or otherwise direct your experience as to who/what you think God is. I have taken a vow of inclusivity to minister to all faiths and none. That means I am open to your lived reality and spirituality or otherwise. The phrase we use is *The God of Your Understanding.* So although I've used quite open terms for the Divine in most of these prayers, if in using the words, you wish to change them to how you see the Universe then please do so.

To prayer itself

A lot has been written about prayer and
it is a subject that will continue to
exercise minds much greater than
mine. There are as many different forms
of prayer as there are faith paths and
people. From body prayers and prayer
songs, to set liturgies - centuries old for
holy days and festivals or rites of
passage. Some prayers bring great
comfort in their familiarity, some may
use phrases or ideas we are no longer
comfortable with (I have a problem with
the Christian word *Sin* but this is not
the moment to expand on that – as I
said there are greater minds than mine
to wrestle with terminology). Equally
some prayers are so beautiful that they
leave us feeling deeply connected to the
Unseen.
Some we utter in a moment of despair
in our own hearts, longing to feel heard
and comforted in our pain. Or prayer
can be for communal joy and
celebration. Or communal sorrow and

remembrance, as a glue for communities or countries to come together when no other response seems appropriate or possible.

I grew up in an English Christian town in that traditional way which meant Sunday school for me and carol services on Christmas Eve for my parents. It's what you did along with a roast on Sundays. Prayer was taught as being a *To Do list for God*. There were people to pray for and maybe a prayer for yourself, but that was usually about your shortcomings (see *Sin* above) or for situations that needed Divine Intervention. It was a lot of talk and rather one way, upwards to Heaven where God sat, with directions and implorings from us to sort things out. That's no longer how I see prayer. I do pray for others; for family, friends and the world, but it is less with an expectation of results. More that I give the names and situations over to the Universe and trust that what is beneficial for all will happen. And it's not for me to direct that – I cannot know what God, or the person concerned has in mind or has agreed to in this lifetime. It maybe that in great suffering the most healing thing would be for a person to pass away, rather than I demand their restoration to health. We cannot know what we are to understand from a disaster or how it will catalyse greater good and love from it. We humans are spectacularly bad at unforeseen consequences of our actions. It might well be disastrous if we could command rain to quench a drought for example – the resulting mud slide could make things much worse. So, I leave it to God and trust.

Prayer for me can be spontaneous – thankful for quiet traffic or a parking space, respectful asking for grace as a hearse goes by. It is part of daily life and almost as natural as breathing. But it is also the beginning part of a quiet time that leads into meditation. I give my concerns to God and then I can clear my mind and heart for a deeper connection that goes some way to quietening the mind chatter.

For me prayer is talking, and meditation is listening. Why is it not obvious that we need to allow the Universe to get a word in edgeways? The answers to our prayers may be there if only we stopped praying for a moment and listened.

Having said all that, I feel that some of these prayers are poems too or just points of contemplation and if you wish to see or use them in that way then that's fine by me.

91

Prayer for when you do not know what to pray

Dearest Whole Love
In your fathomless goodness hold me
close.
Wrap your arms around my frailty and
my weariness.
Know the depths of my heart even when
I cannot find the words.
Lift me up into your compassionate
holding so that I may know your light
and your peace.

And So It Is

For Community Work

As we come together in common cause
We bow our heads and take a moment
of silence.
To learn to listen to all who speak and
all who are quiet.
To learn to speak from the heart to all
who are present.
As we see each other's humanness so
we honour all that each one brings.
So then we are opened to our own
humanness.
In this spirit of humbleness we ask that
You who Loves all
Oversees our work and directs us in
rightful action and ways of peace.

                              And So It Is.

Blessing for an Ancient Site (for West Kennet Long barrow near Avebury)

Ancestors, I approach with a bow,
Honouring the wisdom contained in
these stones
And the stories in the earthy floor.
Your songs are in the air of the passing
breeze.
I give thanks for your lives and those of
the council you kept.
I am sorry that our world is not a better
place than you left it.
You would weep at the destruction
around me.
May I step into your space
With a bow of respect.
May I quietly sit.
May I sing awhile with you.
And pray for a better nature when I am
an ancestor.

And So It Is

For an Old Church

I honour the deep peace of these old
walls and as I walk the aisle I give
thanks for this sacred space.
Blessings on all who are honoured
beneath my feet and on the marble
above.
Blessings of beast and leaf in the
carving skill hidden in corner and
pillar, drift sacred dust down upon the
faithful.
Blessings on the centuries past
worshippers whose bowed heads and
silk rustling dresses still scent the air.
Blessings on those whom you still
shelter in their devotions.
Giving thankfulness for the flower
arrangers and the cleaners
I honour the care and love you bring to
the stained glass of silence here.
May the builders of this place still feel
its work is for the souls it serves.

May the current leaders know their
lineage and in whose footsteps they still
walk.
May it bring peace as I add my prayers
at the altar rail to the God who dwells
in stone and glass and ancient oak.
May the light of Christ and the strength
of the sanctuary door save all who
shelter here.

And So It Is

For Urban Spaces

I drop for a moment into the safe
shelter of my heart – a place quiet of
noise and traffic.
As people rush by, heads bent in their
technology world, so I pray for their
connectedness beyond the metal in
their hand.
May there be shared compassion and
community in the close living of house
and office.
As I watch, I see the human hand of
design in the buildings both old and
new.
I offer gratefulness for bold ingenuity
and patient craft.
But may they not blind us to the Divine
design of the distant hills or the sacred
flow of the river.
I see the robin in the tree and the
beggar in the doorway both taking life
as it is given.

I see the pain behind blank faces, of private struggles masked.
May all find shelter from troubles and peace in the warmth and courage of shared truth.
May the provision that urban life affords not separate us from the vast sky of our belonging to All that Loves Us.

And So It Is.

To Bless a New House

Biding hail and honouring the spirit of
place we ask to step across the
threshold into this new house.
We come with much joy and
anticipation at this new phase of living.
To all that have built this place we offer
thanks for the gift of shelter and
warmth and a place to be nourished
and rested.
May anything that is not in alignment
be harmonised and may all essences of
previous occupants depart in peace.
With loving intent we clear all non-
beneficial energies.
And ask that all elements that remain
will work with us as we are opened to
working with them for the good of All.

And So It Is

For Wherever We Find Ourselves

When I am feeling lost - You find me.
When I am unsure - You comfort me.
When I do not know why I am in this
midst - You find me.
In the great Unknowing of this time so I
sit with the uncomfortable.
In the great Confusion of this time so I
sit with the blindness of humanity.
When I am feeling lost – You find me.
When I am unsure – You comfort me.
When I do not know why I am in this
midst – You find me.
And then there is peace and trust.
And then there is love and compassion.
And then there is hope.
You always bring hope.

And so it is

Gratitude

Often prayer is seen as about praying for resolution of troubles for ourselves and for others. Whilst that is vital work there is much to be said for gratefulness and thankfulness.

Choosing to remember just how much I have got (from health to freedom to material goods) even in the midst of life sets me in to a positive, right frame of thinking. The old adage of *Counting Your Blessings* comes to mind. I was particularly thinking about this as at the time of writing we'd recently moved to a new house. The unpacking of all my clothes, books etc really reminded me just what abundance I have.

Equally as we have walked the local landscape and I've been struck by its beauty, so that has also drawn me to be thankful for the natural world. As I sit

on a stone or a dune and rest my legs
from a walk and soften my gaze looking
out towards the sea, so I am reminded
that gratitude can be a complete feeling
not just in my thinking but the whole of
my being. I feel wholly at peace and
wholly grateful in that moment.

Gratefulness allows me to watch for
tiny birds or find the daisies and pretty
sea glass. That thankfulness is
contained in the wonderous small
details as I breath in the wider view.

In an urban setting perhaps it's as well
to be thankful for parking spaces or a
nice cup of coffee made by someone
else. Perhaps spending even a little of
prayer time being aware of just how
much there is that is positive in life or
even to just say thank you for prayers
received might be a blessing for you too.

Prayer of Gratitude

My Lord
May I look out on this day and see it
anew.
May I notice my breath and the breath
of all beings around me.
I am thankful that I am alive and in
this body in this moment.
I am thankful for all the aliveness that
is in my loved ones and not so loved
ones.
I am thankful for All That Is and All
That Is Now.
May I continue my day bathed in this
soft awareness of gratitude.

And So It Is

Body Gratefulness Prayer

In this timeless moment I draw from my
heart a warmth of gratitude.
It tingles within, rising up to infuse my
smile.
I am grateful
I am grateful.
Closing my eyes to this feeling of
abundance.
Radiating through my crown.
I am grateful
I am grateful.
Down to my feet that are so tenderly
held firm on this earth.
I am grateful
I am grateful.
Allow this feeling to walk with me today
And rest with me tonight.

And So It Is

Prayers for Energy Workers (that means you too!)

So many of us work as healers or lightworkers in myriad ways and modalities. Whilst you may not be aware that you are working as an obvious healer, we live in such times that being aware of the need to offer healing or even just to protect yourself from a sense of something detrimental has become more important. You could say we are all healers now.

If you're not being called to do healing work right now then you might still find these prayers of use as many of us are sensitive to the energies or emotions of others or of places. We may find ourselves going into places or situations with people that leave us drained afterwards and it's not always possible to avoid these scenarios. Or, we might sense that a place makes us feel uncomfortable in some way or even just

that we are in a sacred environment
and want to be respectful.
What unites all the above is a need to
be mindful of all around us and to be
prepared and fully present. Ultimately
it's about taking care of ourselves and
by that I mean all of ourselves, seen
and unseen. It's not fear based - I'm
really not about that, but more about
good *energetic hygiene.*

With all that being said, there is also a
need to setting an intent to begin work
or to prepare to take ourselves in to a
place or situation we don't feel
comfortable about. Having words to
direct our respectful pause can be
helpful.
It is healthy and respectful to
acknowledge we are nothing without
The Source of All or our Guides or
training or whatever it is for you.
Pausing to be grateful for that Divine
presence or knowledge. Taking a
moment to bring ourselves fully to the
present, letting go of life 'out there' so

we are fully able to be with the person/client or situation.
Cleansing our energy fields afterwards and setting ourselves back to 'normal' whatever that means is equally important. It's a way of returning back to the ordinary world, safely and with gratitude.

And in gratitude I offer a deep bow of thanks for the initial ideas from Adrian Incledon-Webber who first introduced me to the idea of protection when doing energy work.

You will no doubt have your own way of doing things but here is my offering in case you don't have that to hand or you want to try something fresh.

Calling in my Power and Truth

I stand before you.
Divine Power of All.
In my fragile humanness I recognise my
weakness.
But with your help I can be All I Need
To Be in this moment and for this work.
Through the bracing of my roots I call
in anchoring earth.
Through the doorway of my solar plexus
I call in sunlight strength.
Through the warmth of my heart I call
in unending love.
Through my crown I call in the healing
that is needed.
May it flow through me and outwards
May I shimmer and sparkle through my
eyes with all I see
And through my mouth with all the
words I bless.

And so it is

Standing Energy back down to Normal

I stand before you.
Divine Power of All
I am grateful for all we have blessed
and healed together.
Now is the moment to let go the energy
you have sent me.
To fold back my wings and put away my
symbols of healing light.
May anything that doesn't benefit me
leave all that I Am.
May I feel refreshed and lifted up from
anything draining.
May I remember to self-care and rest
once this prayer is said.
Closing all portals and anything that
was opened expectedly and
unexpectedly.
Allowing my energy levels to contract to
normal settings
I am at peace and I am blessed.

                        And so it is

Short meditation to begin group energy work.

It is important to be aware when doing any energy work that there can be elements that are detrimental to us. Not to encourage fear but to set our intent mindfully and safely.

Please remain where you are with your feet firmly on the floor and let hands relax by your side.
All is well – breath easily.

Please close your eyes and bring yourself from your head down into the centre of your being.
There in the darkness is safety and peace.
Allow that feeling to wash over you for a moment.

Please bring into your awareness the God of Your Understanding, any guides,

angels or power animals that you work
with.
Ask for their presence and help in this
exercise.
Know and feel that they are now with
you.

Ask that an ultra-fine mesh of love and
light appears and that the angels or
guides take hold of the ends.
Ask that this mesh gathers up and
removes all that is unbeneficial or
detrimental to you including all the very
tiniest of beings.

Beginning at your feet draw this mesh
gently upwards, through your ankles,
knees, thighs and pelvis.
Up through the chakras of your body –
root, sacral, solar plexus, heart,
Feel it cleansing and gathering.
You might see it and or feel what it
gathers.
Continuing drawing up along your arms
and hands.

Through the throat, up through the face
and ears.
Gently cleansing and clearing as it pulls
up and through.
Onwards and up to the third eye and
then beyond crown.
Allow your Divine helpers to gather up
this mesh and carry it off for you
towards the light for the Universe to
release and disperse.

You are safe and at peace.
Feel the freedom of being fully clean
and sparkling.

Now allow your guide to flood your
being with the most beautiful healing
light adding joy and all good things.
Feel that light filter through all of you –
the physical, auric and beyond.
You are completely filled with healing
energy.
You sparkle!
You are a divine and wonderous being.

Feel that healing light and that sense of
safety and peace.
This light forms a wonderful cloak
around you from crown to ground.
You are now fully protected.
Nothing outside can harm you or reach
you.
Please thank your guides and helpers.
And gently return to the room.

Forgiveness

Forgiveness seems such a difficult word and concept now. To ask for forgiveness can be seen as a weakness rather than a moment of honesty and humbleness. People in the public eye have muddied it all with fudged and insincere apologies. I wonder if we trust forgiveness.

I hope we have come away from the idea of a vengeful Divine set to punish us for our wrongdoing, but there is still a place for a prayer to acknowledge in private that which we have got wrong in life.

We are unconditionally loved by the Divine and when we humbly pause and ask for forgiveness then we can feel that lifting of guilt. We can feel that love no matter what. This helps us turn to others who have wronged us and whilst

they may not be able or even aware of a
need to apologise we can begin to be at
peace with that person or situation.
So I offer a very simple prayer for
forgiveness.

Prayer For Forgiveness

With my humble bent head and closed
eyes
I ask that what I have done is brought
before You.
I ask that what I have not done is laid
in front of You.
I ask for the forgiveness of not knowing
where I've fallen short.
When I am honest with You then I
know that I am forgiven.
And I can take that forgiveness out in to
the world and forgive those that hurt
me.

And So It Is

To bring a group to the present after a break.

I invite you to step back into the room from the busyness of outside and from the rush, noise and turbulence of the city.

Find, deep within the mystic heart space of you, a steady calm centre.
The true you.
So, this centre that is you stands firm, holding the beloved husk of the physical.
See how the true and centred you sparkles like the most perfect radiant star.

See how there is a root from this star that extends below the chair, below the floor and down deep within the earth - from which you are made. It is tied (with the most pretty of bows) to a gold bar with your name on it.

Feel that this root holds you steady
whilst the world rocks and swirls on its
axis all around.

Flowing up this root to your centre
again see that there is the whisper of
gossamer thread moving up beyond the
rooves, beyond bird heights, up into the
infinity of the stars - from which you
are made.

Hear the Universe and the stars sing
with the song of your being. They are
the choir of your divinity
Know that you are here in the infinity of
this moment.

And that the true sparkling you stands
firmly anchored to earth and stars.
Take energy from them
Take groundedness
Take song
Take a step forward from this moment
into a deep peace.

                        And so it is.

Prayer for Closure of a Relationship

Our guides and angels hear us when we
pray
When it is time for two to take different
paths we hear the whisper of our hearts
and spirits and we know it is to be.

We stand fully in the truth of all we've
done in this relationship in love and in
less than love.

We ask forgiveness from each other for
any hurt caused.
We are grateful for the honesty of this
moment for healing of the two hearts to
flow.

We are grateful for all we have shared
and all we have learned.

In this moment and by Divine grace we
two together, become two single ones.

We stand separately and grounded in who we are as individuals.

And picking up our bags and with a bow of gratitude we go our separate ways.

May we send blessings for our own journeys and wish the other the fondest of memories.
It is done
It is done.

And So It Is

Prayer for Bereavement

We pray for the loss of our beloved
[*insert name*]
Allowing the tears to flow and our
hearts to be heavy.
We acknowledge the emptiness that is
left.
The hole where our dear one was and is
no longer.
The conversations we cannot now
finish.
The hugs we cannot now share.
Source of All love enfold us in your
care.
Help us then to enfold our family.
Help us to be gentle in these tender
days.
Help us to see safely in the rawness of
grief.
Source of All love bless us as we weep.

And So It Is

The shortest of prayers

I am
And in that I am
Is You.

And so it is

Come be at peace (O silent One)

Come be at peace
O Silent One.

Come be passion
O Beloved One.

Come be Love
O Embraced One.

Come be perfect
O Radiant One.

And so it is

May all that
I Am.
Bless you with
All That You Are.

Acknowledgements

In any new endeavour there is a steep learning curve and producing a book is no less of one. Writing the words was the easy bit. I am delighted to gratefully acknowledge the help I was given.

- To my beloved husband Tim, thank you for patiently helping me particularly with basic IT. Thank you for being the main proof-reader in this house. Punctuation sometimes fails me and your mantra that 'your readers need to breath, Julie' is oft said. Therefore, any complaints of errors of grammar and punctuation found in this book will be addressed to you.
- To Peter Knight and Sue Wallace, fellow writers, dreamers and walkers of the landscape. Your

knowledge and unlimited patient help remain invaluable as I stepped though the portal labelled Self-Publishing

- To all my viewers on Facebook thank you for listening, sharing and commenting on these tender words. Thank you for your encouragement that I was 'on to something'.

- To all at One Spirit Interfaith Foundation – for my gentle and sometimes not so gentle awakening to who *I Am*. Thank you for nurturing the voice within me and helping me learn to trust the Divine even when the leading edge of experience was tough.

To All That Is who holds me and whispers the words within these pages.

Much love always.

Praise for Living Crumbs

This first book of poems by Rev Julie Kirby takes us outside our lockdown world to the weather and the touch of the earth. The poems are interspersed with introductions to the sections, and beautiful photographs of scenes relevant to the themes of the poems, mighty scenery, domestic life and boots all feature.

Julie's writing is clear and rooted in the senses. We can hear the wind, feel the rain, we revel in the sunshine. Julie's physical environment and how it impacts on the inner life is the largest theme going through the volume. We also visit calm domestic contentment, the natural world, love and loss. These, always with an edge of striving for deeper connection with the elements and God.

The Covid poems are darker, but as with all Julie's work, there is an undercurrent of hope. The animal poems (a skylark, a mouse, birds) are honest and do not romanticise nature, but see it.

Many of the pieces take the reader out into the elements in order to find deep solace and peace. Julie's Wales is seen in all its beauty, and also in its folklore in the poems as well as in the photographs.

Prayers are introduced midway through the work, and we are told of Julie's approach to connecting with God. Again, Julie's connections with her environment close to home and further afield inform the rhythm and the depth of the prayers. We are brought to castles, churches and to her own new home. Themes of power, energy and gratitude sit easily in the volume, as these themes are also present in many of the poems. Personal experiences of death, relationship breakdown and forgiveness are all addressed through prayers. These are both beautiful and useful pieces, and *many readers may find themselves connecting with God as they read.*

A beautiful deep, thought provoking book.

Rev. Mary McKeown (MPhil BBS)

This remarkable anthology is a wondrous potpourri of profound reflection, astute observation, and prayers to truly inspire and comfort.'

Peter Knight – (Stoneseeker Publishing)

My lasting memory of Julie is of her leaning against a tree on the banks of the Henge at Avebury in Wiltshire, with her eyes closed, at peace with the world. She and the tree quickly became one, their energies merging in a truly symbiotic relationship. It was very apparent to me that a true and unadulterated love was shared between the two of them that day. For us humans connecting to Mother Earth is equally as important as our uniting with the Universe. We are the natural conduit between the two, inextricably linked to the Divine.

This is what Julie has successfully put into words within this delightful book, helping us to develop a closer relationship not just with the natural world or the heavens, but also, importantly with ourselves.

A true reflection of life.

Adrian Incledon-Webber (Dowsing Spirits)